Susan was born in 1947 in Nelson, Lancashire, where she spent her early childhood before moving to Lancaster at the age of 12. She attended Lancaster Girls' Grammar School and then gained a teaching qualification from Northern Counties College, Newcastle-Upon-Tyne in 1968. Susan has maintained a lifelong passion for both writing and reading poetry.

This collection includes poetry on her favourite subjects, including contemporary people-poems, humour in everyday situations and prose-poems on the natural world. She is currently studying Creative Writing at the University of Kent at Canterbury and lives at Whitstable, with her husband David.

KALEIDOSCOPE

Poetry by

Susan Groom

Kaleidoscope
First published in 2007

Typeset by DJG,
Whitstable, Kent, United Kingdom
Printed in Great Britain

ISBN 978-1-84753-598-6

For my family, especially my husband Dave, for all his patience, help and support in making this happen.

Enjoy!

CONTENTS

MY VENUS FLYTRAP

Carnivorous jaws open, like a Venus Flytrap,
to swallow my life's ephemera.
Like my life, cluttered with screwed-up receipts,
wrappers of sweets, two out of date tickets for the cinema.

An old apple lies at the bottom, might need a snack.
Stabbed and bruised by my hair-brush,
left long forgotten, I look at the fruit bowl,
decide no, I can't put it back.

My favourite lipstick lost deep down under my keys.
I turn everything over, fathom the depths, go down three times,
I'll just have to look pale and interesting,
hope that nobody sees.

A bottle of water was popped in here somewhere,
this rat trap's cavernously big,
it's always handy if I get a headache,
to take pills, in a heat-wave, an emergency swig.

A sodden diary under my fingers,
the bottle leaked into my purse.
In the whale's dark intestines
Jonah could not have felt worse.

I can't go anywhere without it,
rat trap, fly trap, my bag, given so many names,
a sanctuary for my life's belongings,
to show it's insides to others makes me ashamed.

One day soon I'll give it a clear-out, show it I care.
I carry round my very own kitchen sink.
It's a comfort to know it's all there, with a foot-spray
so I'm not the one whose feet stink.

My mobile phone rings, muffled, far away.
Oh God, I can't find it, lost in the lining again.
Gotcha, let me check, yes, you've guessed it,
it's the sixth call I've missed today.

IN CHAINS

You said you used to pull the legs off
insects when you were young.

Now, it's petals off our love, one
by one. Watch me carefully

see my expression,
teach me a lesson. Each daisy,

he loves me. Pain.
He loves me not. Hurt.

When I pick some more and
make a chain

you say I'm a sensitive
flower and no-one's to

blame, but I look and see
the petals lying all around our

feet and it's too late
to start again.

He loves me,
he loves me not.

OLD FRIEND

I've sold my old car for a new one,
parked it up at the garage, left it flat.
Felt a bit sorry, walking away,
took a half-guilty look back.

It wasn't a car to write home about,
just got me around with no fuss.
It never needed repairs or broke down,
leaving me to consider the bus.

The colour wasn't eye-catching,
out of the ordinary, not too bright
It just blended in with the traffic,
especially when I drove home at night.

The wipers worked intermittently,
the electric windows had a mind of their own.
If I pressed the switch once, they went up,
when I wasn't looking, crept surreptitiously down.

Vision was perfect from all angles,
the driving seat felt like a pram.
No electric-assisted steering for this beast,
it just knew where to go, like a lamb.

Of suspension it seemed quite devoid,
I felt every bump and hole in the road,
in a journey, never a dull moment,
all the senses well employed.

Gear changing proved a bit tricky,
a hill start could cause a fright,
as you saw the scenery for a second time,
when the handbrake took forever to bite.

I hear you ask me about this new one.
What's it like, the colour, the make?
Well, my friend, I've just cancelled the order,
bought it back, for old times' sake.

INVASION

A woodlouse treks across the Sahara, my carpet.
Another advances from the opposite side,
high noon for woodlice.
More and more invade like an army every day.
Why choose *my* house to stay?
I let my eyes rove across the desert,
check for wandering nomads with dread,
can't just walk with relaxed abandon, look straight ahead,
watch out for these Tuaregs of the shag-pile,
take care wherever I tread.

Some are very canny, roll up into a ball,
with a woodlouse sixth sense
at the approach of a giant, alien footfall.
Others, the fattest, just keep on trucking,
desperados, machos of the bunch.
Should I sweep them outside,
gourmet treat for local hedgehogs to munch?

Here's another woodlouse conundrum.
Yesterday, with a sinking feeling,
I saw one march across my kitchen ceiling.
Outpost of the battalion,
sent for a panoramic view of the battlefield.
Can't believe my eyes,
a medal to that one, for woodlouse enterprise.

I might give my Dyson its head
to get rid of my armoured friends.
A sort of smoothie of woodlice, start a trend,
but I wimp out at the last minute,
can't let them enter the eye of the storm,
put my hoover away, still with no woodlice in it.
In my insomniac nights, when I don't put the light on,
I can't see where they are.
Without my slippers
I think you'll agree, it might be a step too far.

So we all live together, our symbiosis agreed.
Some scooped up, sent packing out of the door,
others crawl off to their mystery barracks.
Do the same ones come back? I’m not sure.

I might use their movements in the interests of science,
calculate their speed, how far can they go?
Like an eccentric biologist, I take out my notebook,
    start to mumble,
but NO, fetch the mixing bowl out, put the oven on.
Anyone for woodlouse crumble?

SOLITAIRE

I saw her first at the coast
with most of her possessions
in a battered greasy red trolley.
She pushed it before her tenderly,
like a baby in a pram.
Piano-player fingers, nicotine stained,
yellow nails, knuckles tension-white.
Gloria, Barbara, maybe Pam,
patrolling the cafés, promenade and street,
an officer on her beat.
Sharp, kohl-black eyes averted
from anyone she meets.

Shuffling towards me on worn-out
soft brown, wrinkle-booted feet,
she took me by surprise, stopped to speak.
I saw the accident happen, she said.
Heard the smash of glass on post.
Yes, I've taken down the details,
well, I've tried to remember most
of the number and the colour,
but the make of car, no, I can't be sure.

I looked back minutes later,
saw her by a parked-up police car,
leaning in, propped at the open door,
arms gesticulating wildly, telling them more.
Hair long, dark and scouring-pad wiry,
camel coloured coat way down to the floor.

I saw her next in the supermarket,
wandering slowly,
the smell of fresh bread,
keeping herself to herself.
Like a store detective on duty
prowling her shelves,
spotting those who might help themselves.
With only a trolley, streetwise eyes
and some social conscience of which to boast,
alone, vulnerable, one of life’s survivors,
I saw her first at the coast.

PRIMATE CHANGE

Erosion floods our minds,
life sea-levels on the rise,
blows through our brains
the sand of desert places.

Washes past our faces,
an acidic ocean, fields of coral,
slowly bleaching,
leeching, killing.

Bitter thought-water filling
our mouths with dead fish.
We try spitting them out,
deny they are dying,

But still they choke us, lying
rotting, for miles around
under carbon-thickened fog,
autistic darkening grows.

Warm salt-water flows
from rapid ice-berg melt.
We drown in glacial tears,
mourn felled forests, poison skies.

Cover up our eyes,
put hands over ears,
the storm winds
are beginning.

Thoughts are twisters, spinning,
shaking the bars of our rib-cage.
Nowhere left to hide in a
polluted search-lit night.

We stare, minds closed tight,
inside our ebony prison,
wait for our planet, intestate, to die.
Erosion floods our minds.

BROKEN FLOWERS

Shock of flowers at a bus stop,
propped on a graffitied street wall.
For who, why, a stab in the park?
My city, a macabre florist's shop,
too open to the sky, I avert my eyes.

Lilies, daisies, laid with love,
brothers, sisters, tears,
a mother's dropped black mourning glove.
Blood-red roses seen
from my speeding car.
A cross marks where you are remembered
by wounded hearts still here.

Flowers left to help heal the scar,
wither and die, but you,
with bullets and blades,
must try to hide from silvered mirrors,
where splintered reflections look back.
You know who you are.

Too many broken flowers,
sweet, heavy scent of death.
In a one-minute's silence,
I wonder who's to blame.
A black limousine glides past,
I lay my flowers at the wall.

IF YOU ARE A MOUSE

Celebrate your fabled smallness when you hide
from stalking cats or brandished brooms
in gloom of musty sheds.

Let your velvet furriness, in a child's gentle palm,
speak for you, your eyes like jet beads.

Let your perfect claw-feet scamper you
through fields of hissing corn
before the hunting combine.

Be happy for your whiskers.
Let them tell you if it's through
a hole you can sneak.
Tweak your nose, let it give warning,
more time to run.

Enjoy your worm-like tail
for the balance it gives.
It curls around blind babies
in the nest where you live.

Find time to clean the baby-pink
smoothness in your ears.
Be glad they are your radar.

But, remember, you must never
develop a taste for cheese.
The trap lies steely, unforgiving.

Like you, it can move swiftly,
but, unlike you, brings
suffering and sudden death.

HAIKU SYMPHONY

Children run and hide,
moon tiptoes across the sky,
sun strides from the East.

A sun kissed new day,
doors open, birds call, bells ring,
and the sky sings too.

Summer rain washes
petals and leaves with tears from
the face of heaven.

Innocent, pure, white,
Mary Magdelene roses.
I think of the Cross.

Musk scented rose climbs
over the sun-warmed brick wall
where lazy bees hum.

Silver flowers
in the shadows of the night
tremble by the lake.

END GAME

Clean jeans, hair washed,
kids dressed. I could do anything really.
Well, nearly anything,
except your words flash like knives
in the bitter dark, the deep cave
that is my mind.
They fire in a gatling of hail.
Your eyes threaten like pistols
in the starless void,
you and I, wind-up toys,
in the pitiless dawn before battle.

My words whisper like falling snow.
Soundless mouthings in the frail slush
of sullen murk.
They creep in a motley of rags,
to find their keep
on the slag heap of insults,
in the trash-cans of shame.
Confirmation of loneliness for
each, the other's cross to bear.

Our lives chained like fugitives
inside the mad-house walls.
Eyes, staring from skillet-black skulls.
Feet tread the ditchwater of dull
compromise, under cover of cunning.
Our lips tremble like penitents,
two foxes, hunted, in hiding.
Clean jeans, hair washed,
kids dressed, I could do anything really.
Well, nearly anything,
except………………
roll the dice again.

BODY LANGUAGE

From your lips,
a wireless message then

a shrug of laughter from
your shoulders and down

your spine a shudder of
gladness, when

your arms are
round me like a

circle of white. But your
prancing, race-horse feet will

take you away down
a road that runs

straight as
a rifle barrel.

LOST IN THE MOMENT

In a bitter gusting north wind,
unexpected cold snap,
a sudden avian voice
pierces the rushing air.
Sweet aria, sneak preview,
then more, more and more voices
in a dawn opera,
elation of a thousand Springs.
Now, silence.
Of the ghostly choir, no sign,
except my lightened spirits
from that lone bird's first minute,
in a bitter gusting north wind.

EYE LOVE YOU

Twenty four million images in a lifetime,
our eyes – amazing, but true.
Out of these twenty four million,
my favourite one is of you.

OPTICAL ILLUSION

My glasses
are my window on the world.
I keep them filled up.
When empty, my world
becomes slurred.

ADDICT

If I turn the TV to the wall,
will I do more
or nothing at all?
Except stare through a crack
at the wires in the back
and wonder what they're all for.

WITHOUT LOOKING

She bought a host of daffodils,
put them down inside the car.
He said he was so sorry,
he'd poked them in the eye.
Thought they were the gear stick
changed to fourth
and made them cry.

CORPUS CHRISTI

On a hill,
high, in the
terrible silence,
under the bruised sky, an apparition of black lace.
Like its own leaf veins, a skeletal charcoal tree.
Stark naked against the suffering of fast-dying,
blood-stained evensong-light. Remember Golgotha.
One twisted,
accusing finger
points through
a halo of
enshrouding rays.
We look for
healing, weep
and wait,
kneel in
the ashes
under the
congealing sky,
in the terrible
silence,
on a hill, high.

APOCALYPSE

The heart of you is a ghost.

On a Christmas-cake landscape,
crackle-icing cover, a cold to crack stones.
A silent, godless world of limbless
trees and alabaster bones.

The lips of you are a ghost.

Beneath steel ribcages
protecting new growth
on glinting fields of gun-metal light,
I feel the pulse of you.

The hands of you are a ghost.

In black-ice loneliness,
a mist of wanting creeps in the valley.
Low sun bleeds slow warmth
into my barren heart-land.

The face of you is a ghost.

Your hair, a ring of stars, tied with coils of cunning,
scattered like a rosary, suddenly unstrung.
My own eyes become sightless
as the eggs of spiders, when I look to find you.

Myself a ghost.

In the cold glaucoma, dimming my world,
black sheen puddles crack, of a sudden,
beneath my marbled feet
and fate waits at my door with a white finger.

We are all ghosts.

ABRACADABRA

Magic in a vase,
Medusa snakeheads,

blind hoodies, in waiting.
I look away, and see

not whipping tongues or
darting eyes but sudden

trumpets, announcing
multiple births.

With a magician's
shocking speed,

dawn-starburst daffodils
from Medusa snakeheads

in a vase.
Magic!

TRANSIENCE

Zizzing, whizzing, whirring zoomers, the world seems full of hoverflies, tormenting inquisitors, easy-riders, ceaselessly crossing my vision, humming sirens on an emergency mission.

Nature's helicopters, soft amber-striped bodies cleverly keeping perfectly still, alien eyes in sunglasses stare back. I wonder if they can smell perfume, Rougeberry, I think they seem to know.

Like an undercarriage, a long feeler lowers to be cleaned before sudden, final touchdown, on blousy yellow flowers, my dress, a landing pad, resting place for gauzy wings, all motion suspended.

Our paths have crossed, once in a lifetime. We are, for a split second, as one. When he re-zooms his journey, he takes that part of me which longs to fly.

SCENE IN PASSING

When I saw them yesterday, he didn't know
it was grey. I complain every day
when it's grey but he smiles, taps along,
lets his dog find the way.

He might know that it's grey
on a day when he can't feel the sun.
But he still smiles and taps on,
his dog always the one to help him along.

He doesn't know if flowers are there.
Can't tell except for their smell
and the dog doesn't care.
It just stops until it's clear, no cars,
the pair tap across in the grey
he doesn't know is there.

He doesn't know if it's daylight or night,
but passes by, smiling.
The dog never takes fright.
It's his eyes. No surprise then,
he knows when the dog is not there.

When I saw them again today,
it felt just like the sun
had come out from the grey.

DOLLY MIXTURE

FOR ROSE

O, Lumpetty Anna
you were rain-soaked
when he threw you over the wall.
With your spidery eyes,
bright red smile,
you attracted a cow in the field.

It chewed you.
I cried when I saw you again.
Broken neck, dirty dress
saliva-streaked pigtail, unstitched.

An expression of startled confusion,
both you and the cow,
when I chased it off from the ditch,
cried hot tears with No-Head Ted,
then we got you mended.

For years, we were never apart.
O, Lumpetty Anna
I loved you,
mourn the day I lost you,
remember when you and I played.

MANYANA

You're good for me, you know.
Like rockets at New Year in Sydney,
a glass of champagne in the bath.
Like the blue of mid-summer mountains,
whiteness of untrodden snow,
you're good for me, you know.

So, just give me time
to see flower petals opening,
a day on a beach, watching surf rolling in.
Two minutes to buy that one lucky lottery ticket,
with six numbers destined to win.
Then, I'll be good for you, you know.

999

My life is a mess
like the top of my toothpaste tube.

My head, full of holes
like a sieve.
I'm treading on egg shells,
slipping on skins,
demon doubts search me out.
What's the number
I need to remember?
I turn the dial,
but my life will not click,
like the safe in the wall.
When I squeeze the tube,
even that has gone flat.
My life is a mess.
Nine Nine Nine.

My life is a mess.
Nine Nine Nine.

Which service please?

BOGEY MAN

Someone once said,

dreams can make you smile.
Well, not me and not mine.
Check out the next time
you see me sleeping.
That's no smile but
a nightmarish grin.

See my eyes stare back
like pennies and my
teeth flash like bling.
They say dreams
can make you sing,
but not the ones I'm in.
Dreams can make you shout.
That could have been me,
trying to get out.

Someone once said,
dreams can come true.
Well, that *was* me and
listen up when I say,
check out the next time
you see me sleeping.

It *will* happen one day.

FRUIT SALAD DAYS

In a banana-golden sunrise,
silver slow trails to
damp snail shade.

Whirr-whirr of wings on
feathery flight path to
cherry tree nest.

In a lemon renaissance,
my defrosted thoughts
taste of Spring.

REGULBIUM

A thousand years of history
rattle the bars of this page,
to tell the story, monastery and fort,
sentinel towers, a sacred place.
Faced in stone, crowned by a wall walk,
presiding over an invading frothy cappuccino tide,
washing monstrous sugar-cube rocks,
sea-defences, mica winks and spangles
beside shimmering ribbons of oyster beds.

Wind on our faces, sun on our backs,
driftwood, teasel, spiky sea-grass
whisper what they have seen.
A wind farm melts into
the ghostly chill horizon,
seakale shelters in a burned-out store,
flourishing through skeletal ribs.
Fossilised wooden groynes
run zig-zag to the shore.
Rocks, splashed with orange lichen,
nature's paint, trail a crocodile path,
head to tail, to the pier.

Wind on our backs, sun on our faces,
planes breathe a flight path story
across a vellum sky.
A train underlines in marshland below.
Castellated sea-wall shadows
tell us it is time to go home.
Skull sockets of the flint towers
look both ways through
a thousand years of history.

BIRD IN DENIAL

I have watched you,
choosing not to roost
in dark tracery of branches
at night, with those of the same feather.

Trying not to fluff yourself up in winter to keep warm,
but always finding leafless trees
to protect your secretive nest of fragile blue eggs.

Never using your sat-nav intuition,
losing the way home to hungry, begging young.

Shunning, in summer, a splash in cooling stone bath,
avoiding blood-berried bushes
in time of freezing famine.

Seeking always to fly through open doors and windows,
leaving writhing worms on sparkling grass
after drenching rain,
teasing a creeping, prowling cat.

You are always sorry for your sweet song,
that way we can never know you.

Remember that, like you, the world cannot
always sing, but must suffer pain.
I will watch you.

SABOTEURS

Worms
in my garden,
mean decay
for the earth.

Birds
in my garden
mean death
for the worms.

In Spring,
transformation,
rejuvenation.

Working
l**O**ng
hou**R**s
Moving
top**S**oil

H R H

After the soft early morning rain,
a late narcissus
trembles in the keen breeze.

One glistening diamond-drop
clings to windswept petals of golden hair.

A tiara for the princess of Spring flowers,
her own trumpet announces rebirth.

FOR A KING'S RANSOM

Three pintails meet us by the gate,
paddle over coins,
a small fortune thrown under their feet.
Percussion of squawking welcome,
rising cacophony,
fever pitch of flapping wings
and battling beaks.
Gnarled willows' greening hair
drowses on the shoulders of the water.

Five, in sudden flight of fancy,
rising over foaming cascades
onto a looking-glass lake,
shimmering reflections
of ancient yews.
Beyond, the castle broods,
watches, like the Muse,
two mandarins crossing.

Behind them,
fiery rocket trails
flashing crystals, silver-starburst,
dissolving into
glittering diamonds,
a ring fit for Boleyn.
Air like dry, chilled champagne.
Jeroboam of joy.

Strike of blood-red, clinging
to far battlement walls.
Clusters of aconites, waiting for Spring,
snowdrops, like children, nodding chastely
under bone pale birch,
where birds shall later sing
from feathery throats.

The finale – Miss Havisham,
white peacock, in bridal gown,
long veil of delicate lace
and nodding dainty tiara,
fitting adornment in this historic place.
Her male, magnificent, arrogant,
in emerald, lapis-lazuli blue,
sweeps the ground toward the castle,
like Henry VIII, as if, for an execution,
trying not to be late.

TO DREAM, PERCHANCE OF SLEEP?

Like a wolf howls at the moon, I scream for sleep.
Night unravels like a ball of black yarn.
No sign-posts, 'Sleep → This Way.'
Close my eyes.
They stare from sunken sockets into night,
a big soft thing slashed with gashes of light,
embryo creature in an alien world.
I turn round and round, yearn
for elusive sleep, that temptress,
to overtake me.
Dreams, you call. How can I fall
down so steep, counting sheep, still no sleep?

My bones burn. Can I learn to be a pedlar of dreams?
As I walk, it seems
the whole world is asleep,
except for me. My silent soft feet
creeping, keeping a vigil,
the only feet in the world.
Hear the clock tick,
cold bones click, shadows play tricks.
Dreams, where are you?
Drag me in, pull me down,
to where you are.

I need sleep's healing before light comes stealing.
I lay myself down on the altar of darkness,
curl, curl, ever turning into foetal curves.
Prostrate myself at the fountain of sleep,
in deep, sequinned space.
My eyes weep for repose, close,
I go down, in the unfathomable deep.
I drown.
Alone.

WHERE'S MUM?

In smiling, friendly faces,
sitting down for a chat,
in the chink of café teacups
wearing a cherry-red hat.

Sound of voices singing,
in churches and in Halls,
at rummage sales, for church funds,
and in coffee-morning stalls.

In Classic-FM, in cricket
and snooker on TV all day,
a run out in the car,
just for a "look at the bay."

In a bible and a hymn book,
notelets and postcards sent from holiday,
elephants on a mantel shelf,
placed in order, all walking away.

A chair in the summer-house,
to snooze in, hear the birds call,
in woven baskets and pictures
made to put on the wall.

All these bring back fond memories
for me to forever recall.

THE ELEPHANT IN TOWN

(In the style of Roger McGough)

The elephant said to the kangaroo:
Kangaroo,
When I'm coming through
Betta say 'how do you do'

The elephant said to the constrictor:
Constrictor,
Move faster on the floor, boa
Or I'll crush you for sure

The elephant said to the buzzy bee:
Buzzy bee,
Hey there, can't you see
Quit trying old man, you'll never sting me

The elephant said to the hyena:
Hyena,
OK, your shape is much leaner
And your ways are much meaner

The elephant said to the porcupine:
Porcupine,
To roll in a ball will suit you fine
If you're lucky you'll escape these tusks of mine

The elephant said to the flamingo:
Flamingo,
Though I can't speak your lingo
I just lurrve those legs, by jingo!

The elephant said to the butterfly:
Butterfly,
My dear, as you flutterby
I'll give you a wink with my little eye

The elephant said to the rhinoceros:
Petula,
Give my love to Shulah,
Tracey, Kevin and Yula.

LIKE TRACEY EMIN

Follow your dreams, be a poet they said,
but first, better get out of bed.
Where shall I write then?
Down the garden, in the shed,
only fed through a crack in the door,
dog asleep on the floor.
Might work for a day, I suppose.
Write on a bus maybe, was their plea,
that could be OK, until they wash
it away, with a polishing cloth
so that no-one can see.

Up on a mountain-top blue,
now that's an idea for you, perhaps.
Search on the Internet, spread out your maps.
Just think, at the summit,
you could compose all day,
but I have to say, if a storm came up,
my words might plummet,
paper blown far away.
How about down a cave then
way down deep, under the ground?
Surely there, with no sound,
you could be, in quiet
contemplation of a nation,
with no interruptions for coffee or tea?

No, a dark world, would disturb,
and perturb me, I'm sure.
Too much isolation, for all this creation
and from depression I could need a cure.
So let's see, at the station,
or air-port while waiting.
Write in a café that'll work, they all said.
Get you started, inspire you;
all those people to study, observe
and get into your head.
No, I'm afraid that it won't,
I'm not able, you see.
Never could be, never would be, I said.
To tell you the plain honest truth,
I'm much happier left
picking crumbs from my navel
writing <u>HERE</u> in my UNMADE BED!!!!!!!

TOO LATE

(In the style of Edward Thomas)

Over the sea, speckled with sun and one white bird,
the droning helicopter could be heard,
seeing from sky, blue as a sapphire crown,
what we below could not see,

a child drown.

PETER CUSHING'S VIEW

At day's end, we sit and see bruised ochre in the West,
over shot-silk water, horizon gashed
with streaks of rose-madder white.

Birds in black skeins cross last azure stains.
At our back, fast-fading forget-me-not light
fills with ink-jet clouds, spread wide across the bay,
blotting out and dropping low, over sienna sun-ray.

Tungsten-grey, wind-lapped waves,
gloom-grow, slow-flow, moon-show,
last notes on sky stave.

LINES ON A STATUE

Elegant ivory innocence,
deaf, dumb, and cold
but party to all done and told.

A still, Grecian water carrier,
shows strength and meekness,
no unguarded weakness,
think what story might unfold.

Surely a strand of her hair
could easily fall
on to her humble face,
finely chiselled nose.

Over eyes barely closed,
then from her lips,
do I hear such sweet sighs?

Sinuous, sinewy, one arm,
one leg, bent in deep repose,
jug held gently, she waits to fill

her hand-clasped bowl,
with silent tears.
Smooth drapes waterfall
to her long bared toes.

No shoes for her,
as she silently goes
back into deep thoughts
of sunken archipelagos.

Again, I think I hear her sigh,
long and low, and wonder,
if her sister in the garden with her,
might also softly go.

I'M DYING TO TELL YOU

Would you like some nice hot tea?
No, can't you see,
I'm too busy ……….dying.

Have you got any pain?
Yes, it drives me insane,
and it feels like I'm……….dying.

Can you get into your chair?
No, please not there.
You see, I can't, when I'm ……….dying.

Will you swallow this medicine dear?
Yes, if it's clear,
that I'm still busy ……….dying.

Can you drink from this cup?
No, I can't sit up.
It's too much, when you're ……….dying.

Did you open your bowels today?
Yes, I can say,
that it felt like I'm ……….dying.

Did your husband come in and stay?
No, he passed away yesterday,
so, let me follow, by ……….dying.

Is it you, far away on the phone?
Yes, mum, I'm at home.
Hello, hello, I can't hear, speak up, love, I'm ...dying.

Is this lady getting better nurse?
No, doctor, I'm afraid she's worse.
Well, we'd better tell them, she's ……….dying.

BAY-JA VIEW

'Sea Belles,' 'Happy Days,'
'The Coven,' 'Dragon's Den,'
Beach huts in summer, await owners again.

For the key in the door when a child shouts, *'Yes, it's still here!'*
And runs expectantly out, with a net, to the pier.

'Fortitude,' 'NuttaHutta,'
'Sybil,' 'No Ties,'
Proud sentinels against summer-washed skies.

Blue, yellow and candy-stripe, purple, cream and pale green,
Summer memory-makers in an ever-changing scene.

'Life Begins At,' 'WhyBotha?'
'Layabout,' 'Bay View,'
Sky scuds fast, from pale grey to azure blue.

Children run round them, yapping dogs cock their legs.
When tea has been supped, out fly the dregs.
Broken chair left outside, waste bins piled high
From last nights barbecue, watching fireworks fly.

'St Luke's,' Whitsend,'
'Mango Tango,' 'No Cares,'
Folks snooze in dark doorways, relax in deck chairs.

In Spring, some wait for new paint to be splashed on.
Others lean drunkenly over, for bigger repairs to be done.
Rainbow wind-socks unfurl, twirl in a whipping-cool breeze.
Long-tailed kite flies high on the slopes, dips, drops, misses trees.

'Off-Line,' 'Halcyon Days,'
'Love Shack,' 'Sun Spot,'
Favourite haunts, an escape, time out, work forgotten.

Beach huts in a time-warp, a lost bygone age,
Sticks of rock, jellied eels, buckets and spades.
Today, smoke rises from huts knocked down in a day,
Splintered memories spiral, drift far away.

"To make way for the new," is what I've been told.
But I loved *'Bay View'* in golden sunshine days of old.
Now, it's jet-skiing, speedboat racing or skateboarding on the prom,
And it's *'look out!' 'jump back!'* fast, when bikes speed along.

So, 'SunBeam,' 'Letl Moira,'
'Hotel Splendido,' 'Reverie,'
I'll remember you for ever in these smiling snap-shots of ....

Mum, Dad, Grandpops, Beth, Tommy and me.

DESTRUCTIVE LOVE

Salt-swished, wind-whipped, sun-kissed sea.
Waves lash at the door of memory.
Open, go through, remember with me.
Take my hand, cross the sand
to days of grass-spiked, dust-blown,
slip-slide, run and hide.
Can you smell the sea?
You and me, an ebb-flow memory.

Bucket and spade, flags flying over sandcastles made,
can you see you and me
on a sparkle-bright, white-light day at the sea?
Shell spy, towel dry, gull cry, can you hear
crystal clear water near you and me?
Long-lost memory, of the sea, the sea.

Put a shell to your ear, can you hear? Listen to me.
That gloom-boom, oar-roar,
hiss-kiss of the sea, the sea, still-life memory.
Swim through, you and me want more, push on the door.
Be strong in the curl-swirl, turn-churn,
lash-crash of the sea, the sea.

Tide turns, my heart yearns,
for the memory of you and me, at the sea, the sea.
Caves echo to our calls, 'yoo-hoo, you-hoo.'
In cavernous, slime-sloshed, weed-washed, dark halls
a boat slides through a far-off memory
of you and me, at the sea, the sea.

Leave the boat, take a breath, dive, go down with me.
Can't swallow, must follow,
past life flash, treasure stash, light gash,
until you and me become free with the sea.
You will see, come with me,
once, twice, three times.
to our carefree, lost-love, flash-back distant memory,
of that day at the sea, the sea.

COFFEE LANGUAGE

Frothy cappuccinos,
buzzy, chatty, on the go.
Latte, laid back, wishy-washy flow,
Macchiato, rich, determined.
Espresso, strong, undiluted,
Mocha, smooth like velvet.
Filter, never falter, take their time,
Americano, brash and pushy,
tell their story for a dime.
Smooth, laid back, rich, loud,
read the coffee people,
when you’re in a crowd.

LIFE CYCLES

We have as long as our ticker goes.
Just that long and no more.
Like a washing machine programmed
For so many washes until we're scaled up,
Can't open the door.
Some of us work on a delicates wash,
Take it easy, stay cool, live with care.
Others heat up to boiling point,
Live life in the fast wash, for a dare.
Main wash stay down the middle,
Never deviate left or right, keep on trucking,
Whatever gets them through the night.

Pre-wash are different, take extra time.
On programme one, they can't quite
Get going, push the next button, move on.
Economy always a struggle, trying to make
Ends meet. In hot water, tangled, a muddle,
All washed up, out on the street.
When a crisis gets some folks upset,
They could stay on rinse-hold forever,
Unless someone trips them to re-set.
Many by-pass every wash setting, lose the plot,
Get in a spin, faster and faster,
Make a crazy din. On a quick wash, they never
Catch up, change the state they are in.

One set have it all sorted. Wash, dry, the lot!
Confident, laid back, dried flat.
Freshly laundered, hung in a gale.
Should we envy or tell ourselves
They sometimes get lime-scale.
But, some troubled souls
Lose their bearings,
Ask what does this life mean?
When family and friends check the label,
Find, too late, it says, Special Needs - Dry Clean.

GONE

My heart, heavy like a stone,
when you’ve gone.
Feeling empty and so alone
now you’ve gone.
No voice on the phone,
when you’ve gone.
Aching to the bone,
now you’ve gone.
I must atone,
when you’ve gone.
So much left undone,
two become one,
you’re second to none.
My heart, heavy like a stone.
when you’ve gone.

BLOOD ROSE

Paper-pink, pale petals,
tied round with misty
mercurial ribbons of sunrise.
See the January rose,
how she still grows, on barbed stem.

Blushed with success to be
a delicate refugee from summer
and fragile hostage of winter.
Frozen in time,
granted a last chance to dance.

When stopping to pick her, I take care,
not to prick a finger,
lest I see my blood flow,
like the loss of your love,
so shocking on the snow.

KALEIDOSCOPE

Like splintered emeralds,
the grass glints in sunlight,
spiky as hair on
earth's crusty scalp.
Keeping it warm,
waiting for Spring to
fling up a prism of pansies,
a palette of crocuses,
kaleidoscopic tulips,
like a well watered rainbow.

TRUTHSAYER

To see or not to see into the future?
Whether it is better to leave
A no-mans land of hidden secrets,
Distant clean country of forbidden fruits.
Shall we take the chance,
Consult a crystal ball in the caravan,
Or do we hold the future in our own hands?

Can the two-way traffic of our hand and brain
Give arcane messages in this world from a darker terrain?
Will the Heart Line, the Fate Line, or Line of the Sun
Tell the story in the film of life, not yet run?
See the Finger of Jupiter and Solomon's Ring,
Maybe riches ahead but beware of the sting
In the tale to be told by the Mount of the Moon.

The past, sprinkled with flowers and headstones,
Lies cold and hard beneath us.
History behind, the future unknown,
When we seek to find the secrets of tomorrow.
Shall we lift a corner of the safety curtain today?
Do we dare to see light, darkness or
Loud silence in deep eternity?

Our planet choked by gases, ice-floes long since melted, forests felled.
We have all watched, listened with eyes,
Ears, lips tight-sealed never to tell.
Is there still a chance for wounds to be healed?
Whispers in the night speak a murder of words. Will they be heard?
We carry them away in a kit-bag of shame.

Our planet is threatened. A somnambulist, heading
For the cliffs of destruction like a runaway bride,
Uncertain of her future, why to the altar she came.
Will we hear the bell toll softly
As we walk with arms outstretched?

Wake up. Look around. Seek answers now!
In the stultifying air, a lone bird calls,
'It's not too late....it's not too late,'
Who is to blame when earth's bride
Throws her flowers behind her?
See where they fall.
There, in blood, will be my name.

A 5-7-5 CELEBRATION

Sun burning my eyes,
asking questions in my head,
sinks in blood-red West.

Bush fires rage and burn,
wind fanning flames like bellows,
scorched earth needs our tears.

Cat creeps slowly to
pounce on a singing blackbird,
last notes die away.

Two black swans circle
round a pool of light on the
deep, darkening moat.

A pheasant runs out
and bright red blood oozes on
to the damp, dark road.

Memory is the
camera of my mind and
throws light on the dark.

CONCH-IOUSNESS

On the slow sinking sand of insomnia,
a deep swelling sea,
washes lazy over pebble thoughts.
Shutters gently like shingle,
with the ebb and flow,
onto the beach of memory,
fills pink shells with dreams
before
unconsciousness.

TILL DEBT US TWO PART

On the slow sinking sand of insolvency,
a deep, swelling sea,
washes lazily over penny thoughts.
Shutters gently like cash,
with the ebb and flow,
onto the receipt of memory,
fills the shingle bank with dreams,
before
uncoin-ciousness.

LOVE'S FACES

Love's faces are many, enemies few,
delicate as flowers, transient as dew.

Perplexing as a puzzle, simple, like a child's song,
fleeting as mist, or, as rock, enduring and strong.

Open as a smile, closed as a book,
begun with a warm embrace, or ended with a look.

Fragile as sunshine, in a deep mountain pass,
soft as a whisper, or splintered like glass.

Whatever love is, one thing remains true,
love lives within me, to be given to you.

ANTICIPATION

Berry-bursting bushes
of powder-blue hue,
frame field lookouts,
on a changing year's view.

Skimming clouds cross pale sunlight,
blown by first whispering chill,
wind chimes move in branches,
which, in summer, hung so still.

Crisp carpets of gold,
under bird-speckled skies,
are both heralds of Autumn
and winter's first spies.

PROMISE

Cats slink across the street,
vanish swiftly into shadow,
on foggy-light feet.
Black velvet night
steals blue gauze of day,
banishes last light,
from steely, cold grey.
Crackle-fingered frost,
chills the mind,
the soul, the face,
tracing silent patterns
in crevice, gap and space.

Bulbs stir, await rebirth.
Shoot into sunshine,
from slow-warming earth.
Gold satin light
lengthens silky, silver day,
banishes long night,
from dishwater grey.
Lamb-bedecked fields
promise bright verdant days.
My heart warms
as I gaze.

MY CHERRY TREE

Like a prayerful maiden
begging humble forgiveness,
my cherry tree
hangs her branches
to look at the earth.

White flowers for confession,
and, for nuptials, scatters confetti-pink.
Pleasure-giving, rustle-making,
shade-cooling, bird-song giver,
a little tree, but, to me,
of such great worth.

SETTEE OR NOT SETTEE
- 21st Century Woman

They called her a couch potato,
said deep-couch thrombosis would get her one day.
She lounged on, smoking, drinking,
said they'd come to see things her way.
Plumped the cushions, slid lost coins out,
kept biscuit crumbs at bay.
They said it was the height of degradation,
never going out of the house.
She was happy with TV doofer,
watching news, cuddling her spouse.

Between DVDs and horror films,
she rang the catalogue, ordered clothes.
Enjoyed a TV dinner, drank tea, coffee,
or chocolate, whichever she chose.
On her leather throne, she settled arguments,
sang at the top of her voice,
wrote a poem inside a birthday card,
for a Friend Reunited called Joyce.
She planned for births, deaths,
weddings and christenings galore,
family, friends, dogs and kids
sitting round on the floor.

Laptop balanced on arm, she checked travel times,
fancied St Tropez.
Looked at Emails, cried when one told her
Uncle Tom had passed away.
She chose Peking style
from the local Jade Garden, Mandalay.
Painted her nails red,
swung her legs up, filed her toes,
put her head on the cushion, nodded off,
for as long as who knows.

She flicked through satellite channels,
learned history, how to cook, dance an ice-spin.
Rang her vote through to X-Factor,
saw her favourite singer win.
Raised her glass in celebration,
thought next year she might try.
Got the number, filled the form in,
said she'd post it by and by.
Pressed the red button for weather,
over the next five days,
said she might walk the dog whilst sun lasted,
then brush up on Shakespeare's plays.

From there she could look out the window,
see the post and the milkman arrive.
One day her daughter, out on her pony
tapped at the window, what a surprise!
She sat up quickly, horse's head looking in.
Fed it some jelly babies then the pair trotted off,
knocking over next door's wheelie bin.
If she felt ill, a blanket came down.
With pills and hot tea, she felt better,
curtains drawn, mute sound on TV.

This went on for some twenty years,
cushions flattening, leather cracking and thin.
Suddenly, one morning, he sat down with her,
used his phone, an ambulance took her in.
Whatever she died of, poor old girl,
her lounge epitaph reads,
FROM HER COUCH SHE RULED THE WORLD.

COMPATIBILITY

She was a taxi driver,
he was an undertaker.
They both needed time.

She was an artist,
he was a photographer.
Are you getting the picture?

AUGURS OF WINTER

Remember, remember blood-red poppies of November.

A path fingers through the forest, leaves flutter like tarot cards surrendered from the tree of life, portents, omens, harbingers of winter, wooed by a seducing wind. Red butterfly, migrant bastion of summer, traces a flickering, flutter-by flight path, last admiral of the fleet, sucks ebbing life from a moan of white blossom. Earth spews shocking red agaric that hides between sheltering trunks, tempting the careless and unwary away from the path, dalliance with death the price to pay.

Crossing rain-rinsed storm clouds, the cawing voices of a murder of crows. I think of a Roman augur, in toga of scarlet stripes and purple border, wooden staff pointing skywards, seeking signs in the sky. No flight of eagles or vultures now, but scattering feathers of marauding magpies, a chacking cacophony. The secretive path passes a dank, dark pool, where a balancing boatman skims over the skin of stagnant water. Tangerine-lichened logs bar my way. I retreat from rusting railway remains; the grotesque, dancing shadows of a winding wheel, testament to a bygone era, buried deep in this way through the woods.

A cinder track marks memories of steam, carrying a cargo of coal to the coast. Under trembling trees, I mourn the passing of a ghost. Shiver-shaken, wind-blasted branches etch their tracery, on a Tyrian purple sky. Burning applewood sends smoke-signal memories of an ailing, brown dormouse popped into pocket, hurried back home. Young eyes learn early that life can mean loss. I taste again my salty tears, flowing freely in a garden, beside a small wooden cross hung with daisy chains.

Mist of memories, smoky sorrow, aching angst. Poppies, sentinels of summer in killing-fields of corn, seeds now buried in deep tombs beneath scarred, furrowed iron-cold earth. The wheel of life keeps turning, renewal must wait.

Remember, remember blood-red poppies of November.

GLOBAL WARNING

My own restlessness mirrored by the storm wind,
telling and tapping an S.O.S; Save Our Seasons,
strangely altering death and rebirth,
a global warning, if we but listen to our planet earth.

Battering winds, whipping, wooing and seducing the trees,
then spewing a smoke-screen of starlings,
to be carried on its shoulders, high,
turning, dipping, melting away, lost to the lowering leaden sky.

A taste of 'Black Orchid' gloss lipstick from London,
delivered today, in a van, by a man, blown suddenly sideways.
Now a purple balloon comes dancing, swooping high and low,
swirled far from the party gate, so now, how will children know
    where to go?

Large box, little lipstick, all that fuel, I feel guilty,
sometime, maybe soon, it's a price we will all have to pay.
"Global warming?" Our shouts are lost in the gale,
"That's what they say!" Then, engine revving – it's one more
    sale.

I hear the same dark message come down my chimney,
roaring, moaning, whispering, reaching down,
pointing sooty black fingers of blame.
But will I really listen? Am I going to feel any shame?

Close my eyes, close my ears, close my heart and my mind,
could global warming end every child's party game?
The purple balloon dances one last tango before
we lose one more chair and shut the door.

MINIMA MAXIMA SUNT

See a rainbow not the rain,
hold a baby after the pain.

Smell dew before the day,
kiss a lover who goes away.

Hear bells before the song,
taste tears that make you strong.

Feel whispers of wind's soft breath,
touch a heart between birth and death.

THE 8th WONDER

He said he was into ruins,
the wonders of the world.
That's when I started to wonder
is that why he's with this old girl?
He said he'd seen the Temple of Artemis,
as well as the Statue of Zeus.
That's when I started to wonder
how could I make my excuse?

He said the Hanging Gardens of Babylon
reminded him of my hair.
When he mentioned the Lighthouse at Pharos,
I knew I could never compare.
By the Colossus of Rhodes he seemed fascinated,
more than anyone he'd ever dated.

The pyramids in Egypt,
made him think of my teeth.
That's when I started to wonder
should I have chosen his younger mate Keith?
After many years talking of History,
this artefact saw time going past us.
So I told him one day, in no uncertain way,
I wished him in the Halicarnassus!

WISH YOU WERE HERE

Now, crowds have drifted away,
left the shore-line to seagulls,
screaming high in the heat of the day.
No visitors strolling, sitting,
gazing away out to sea.
Locked beach huts, blind-eyed and boarded,
wait for next year's turned key.

People have travelled back home.
No music, no laughter, no shouting,
from chip-eating trippers long gone.
On the beach, cold sea creeps inwards,
melting castles left by children now back at school.
Over pebbles piled by turnstones,
washing crabs and small fish from their pool.

Memories left far behind.
Wrappers and newspaper litter
piled high under rolled-back blinds.
The carousel stands empty,
golden horses gallop on.
Stalls, lonely and windswept,
wait for bears to be won.

Anguished waves smash the sea wall,
soak the unwary with spray.
In a bandstand where no music lingers
tramps shiver down low from gales,
breathing warmth onto bone-cold fingers,
no interest in Christmas or sales.

Southern breezes turn milder,
post-equinox lengthens the day.
When the coast has been washed by the breakers,
and the sky reflects blue from the grey.
When the caller shouts, 'Bingo!' and tills ring
they'll return for their annual stay.

NO TEARS

Hum and buzz of voices,
a strident bell marks out the day,
from this familiar place, full of life,
hard to stay away.

Children, parents, teachers,
moving to and fro,
each day very different,
so much to learn and know.

Shared laughter, fun and secrets
sometimes anger, maybe tears,
a problem, discussed,
soon disappears.

A place of healing and calm,
through prayer, story and songs,
where every child can feel special, safe,
knowing he belongs.

Now, for me, at home, with
many fond memories,
I remember all of these
small faces, smiling eyes.

No tears, you say?
But I reply,
How can it be
otherwise?

A LITTLE GEM

Through emerald leaves,
a citrine sun shone
on the diamond lake,
from a sapphire sky.
It was a jewel
of a day.

ALPHA TO OMEGA AND BEYOND

We are all grains of sand in the hour-glass of time.
We must march beyond blood and bones at our birth.

When the hourglass turns, the shifting, sifting,
life layers run through.
How quickly run the crystals of time for you?
Can you tell? Do you know?
Some black, some white
and a rainbow of colours to show.
Some grains run through days sent from heaven,
others through days of our own hell,
always shifting, sifting,
ever-running through ageing fingers,
never stopping, always dropping,
grains of crushed mountains and shell.

Can we ever take control? Could we ever keep control
of the trickling crystals of minutes, days or years?
But keep moving, don't look back, cross the ever-shrinking,
sinking sands of time, always falling, never stalling.
Can we count the grains?
Is their number the same for you and I?
We cannot know, even if we go,
to kneel and howl in the wilderness,
on the wild blue mountain,
scream into the stabbing storm,

I hear no merciful answer and return to the foothills.
Through piercing wind, forked lightning,
back to lanterns of home, under drifting, shifting sky,
beneath the cold, poised axe-blade of time.
Shall I look to the heavens through sun's molten bars?
or lift the cool cloak of midnight?
Would one way be wrong, the other way right?
Past meteors, shooting-stars and falling comets.
If mankind shall survive, then another star calls.

Look now or look then, I cannot say when,
even if we cry to the sky, to the blue or the black,
the hourglass can never, ever, be turned back.
Start again, I ask? No, it is not in my power to intervene,
or have a pardon before the legal midnight hour.
Should I count the grains? Can I know?
Did I get the right hour-glass?
I want you to show, was it the right one?

How to tell?
Maybe mine for that of another's I might consider to sell.
What if the hour-glass with elephants was filled?
A short life that would surely be.
But no, maybe one that's much longer
as they'd all be stuck fast, never to be set free.
What if my hour-glass with raindrops was filled to the brim?
Would my life have ended before it could begin?

If the drops turned to ice, then for me,
time could stand perfectly still, frozen in days, months and years.
I could return and watch the world for ever,
from that far-distant blue hill.
An hourglass filled with marshmallow-soft clouds
may hold back time just for me, but all too soon,
I can see they too will start drifting, sifting, gliding, hiding,
sailing by in silence, to be lost in my memory.

But now I must walk, sometimes stumble and run,
glass turning, heart yearning,
midnight's black cloak gathered around me
when I was not looking, pinned back by sequinned stars.
I run and hide under gathering clouds
in the fast-lowering twilight, not looking up or back,
lest they drop, until, beyond this blood there is only dust,
our own dust, shifting, sifting, and drifting.

To be sprinkled o'er red and white roses so sublime,
High on a far-distant blue hill, from the now-stilled
hourglass of time.

HIDE AND SEEK

Under rosy-tinted clouds of childhood,
running through long lavender shadows, throwing pennies.
Each, a trophy of remembrance, a secret wish.
See the child under the bridge,
dancing with curly hair in the pearly glare.

Suffused in the faerie glen of memory.
Tin-foil sunlight filters
through a litany of running water
onto granite-shining rocks below.
I see myself go, under fountain flow,
to throw childhood pennies, lost, long ago.

Rainbow prism flashes through trees.
I watch, hide in a stone-silent, vesper-cool temple,
where I fall on my knees,
close my eyes, hardly breathe,
until I hear shrieking, seeking voices,
"Coming! Ready or not!"

Count to ten, look again, whirling twirling,
two girls laughing, in long purple coats,
never stop dancing together.
Quicksilver splinters on the scrying-glass lake.
Two ballerinas,
after-images in a musical box, eerily turning forever.

In the tranquil shade of the waterfall glade,
secret place we have made.
Follow the path, winding and finding its impetuous way,
past fountain, temple and bridge, in breathless silence,
to the folly, to the folly
where once was a quarry.

In the low blue lustre, we slip, trip, run down
slab-cold steps, to the sun-dial,
its hour-points laid round an ellipse,
to be gnomons, skipping round the circle of youth,
small seekers of answers, purity and truth,
when happiness was cheap.

Sullen sun has melted low,
moon's milk-white wishing-disc will show.
Time knocks in another nail, the cycle of ebb and flow.
For a while, I smile, rewind the spool,
find a different me; innocent, running free.
I hear you say, *"throw a coin in the fountain today."*
You know what my wish will be.

Coming! Ready or not!

FOLLYWOOD

In rhododendron groves, lustre of storied estates,
in shade of cedar, beech and cypress,
redbrick mansions, gracious homes to
screen sirens, marinating movie stars,
glitzy glamour and passion.
Regency staircase, in mock-Georgian manor,
entrance for divas, darlings and
doyennes of red carpet fashion.
Solace from the city,
show place, a tale of two faces,
the private, the public,
art needs to breathe, my dear,
have a pulse, don't you know?
In ornate silver jug, white peonies, rose-tipped, full-blown,
firework glow of deep blue delphiniums,
exuberant, sumptuous, while above, the crowning glory,
crystal chandeliers, delicate, antique,
stylishly sparkle their story.
Iconic gowns, the public face, smiling,
to so much applause, translucent, diaphanous,
plunging chiffon, ruined at the Oscars darling,
snagged, pulled and stepped on.

An old school glamour goddess sits, her day done,
in silver-wallpapered gloom of her luminous room,
with mohair, velvet, leather, cashmere and silk shantung.
No public face for years, she sits and she stares,
in her museum, mummified, modified, customised.
Hair, poodled-up, a Velázquez Infanta,
staring out, beyond her veranda,
to another vista, grand and grander.
Art needs to breathe, my dear, have a pulse, you know.
The black phone hangs off the hook,
a small bright voice tinkles, "Hello darling…Darling….hello……..?"
More bourbon, more water, more tablets,
she watches a tear slide and go,
to sit with the diamonds on her evening sandal,
silently, oh so slow.
Her sun's fiery orb drops over a turquoise horizon.
Like a candle, planet Venus twinkles low
and her moon leans down to watch over Tinseltown.

THE LEAF TURNS

Now is the time when
plants bloom, vibrant with new growth
in syrupy sun.

Shoots of Pieris,
red drama queen, Forest Flame,
dressed to kill and thrill.

Look, drooping clusters,
pure white flower panicles.
How fresh the new leaves!

Now is the time when
birds tell their story to a
watermelon sun.

JUST ONE MORE

FOR MUM

If only
you could have seen
just one more daffodil day.
Looked at just one more
glittering bay and had
just one more cup of tea,
served on a pretty tray.

If only
I could have found
just one more way
to say, I love you
and please stay.

If only you could have seen,
just one more.

If only……….

www.ingramcontent.com/pod-product-compliance
Ingram Content Group UK Ltd.
Pitfield, Milton Keynes, MK11 3LW, UK
UKHW012246240726
13966UKWH00004B/1314